WHY
insurance
companies
HATE
when you hire
a lawyer.

New York City Accident Victims:

WHY
insurance
companies
HATE
when you hire
a lawyer.

RICHARD C. BELL

**The Law Offices of
Richard C. Bell**

545 8th Avenue, 8th Floor
New York, NY 10018

(877) CALL-LAW
www.877calllaw.com

ISBN: 978-1-63385-330-0

Designed and published by
Word Association Publishers

205 Fifth Avenue
Tarentum, Pennsylvania 15084
www.wordassociation.com
1.800.827.7903

Dedication

This book is dedicated with love to those who have made my wonderful and rewarding legal career possible - my lovely and forever encouraging wife Florence, my incredibly supportive late parents Esther and Ben and late grandparents Sam and Annie, my lawyer role model brother Alan, our very special dogs Bingo and the late Sadie, my very fine late mother-in-law and father-in-law, Taka and Frank, my very strong and courageous late cousin Arnie and late friend Russ and the most dedicated and smart paralegals ever, Liz and the late Jazz.

Important Disclaimer and Warning

■ ■ ■

This book is intended to supply you with some general information if you are an accident victim or a family member/ friend of an accident victim. No legal advice is contained in these pages. I am not your attorney until and unless we enter into a written retainer agreement that clearly spells out an attorney-client relationship. Ordering or reading this book does not create an attorney-client relationship. If you wish to contact me to discuss a potential case, please call me at 877-CALL-LAW (877-225-5529) or (212) 714-0988 to discuss whether or not your potential case merits an in-person, free consultation. Every case has its unique facts and circumstances so I cannot render any legal advice to you until we establish a written attorney-client relationship.

Contents

one
The Author's Inspiration - **You**

For the past 37 years, I have had the honor of representing accident and medical malpractice victims in their fight for justice. As a trial attorney in New York City, I have fought on behalf of those injured and killed as a result of motor vehicle accidents, falldowns, construction tragedies, defective products, police brutality, medical malpractice, nursing home negligence and other accidents caused by another's negligence.

The one constant in my professional career is the inspiration provided by my clients. Those that I have fought for were truly victims up against powerful insurance companies representing large trucking companies, supermarkets, landlords - both corporate and individual, the City of New York, the U.S. Government, national and international construction companies, major manufacturers, well-known hospitals, doctors and nursing homes. Many times, it did seem like David against Goliath, but no righteous fight is ever won without a constant battle. As Ghandi once said, "First they ignore you. Then they laugh at you. Then they fight you. Then you win."

My clients have had some of the most unfair events imaginable change their lives forever in an instant. A car accident caused by awful road design and maintenance took my infant clients' parents away forever. Industrial machinery took away a client's arm. Medical malpractice by a doctor took away most of a client's penis. A truck caused a young client's neck to become so seriously injured that his physical and emotional enjoyment of life was crushed. A raised street grate caused a falldown that ended a client's career and severely limited his ability to walk forever. Dangerous construction scaffolds and loose planks have caused irreparable harm to my construction worker clients just trying to do their jobs. A young parent of two died at a major New York City hospital because the doctors and nurses were negligent in failing to diagnose a respiratory condition that was completely reversible if diagnosed timely. A supermarket delivery man can never work again because a loading dock worker removed a ramp while the deliveryman was inside the truck and the gap created by the missing ramp caused my client to fall and sustain a permanent neck injury. These preventable catastrophes are what I see every day, but I never get used to the human toll they take on my clients.

All of these tragic accidents have common elements. Each client hired me to mount a fight for her/his rights against well-financed, powerful entities backed by insurance companies that devoted enormous resources and skilled lawyers to deny my clients any money for pain and suffering and lost wages.

Each client was aware that the battle would not be easy, would not be short and would not be a straight line to victory. These brave clients did not spend their time simply waiting for the lawsuit. No. Their time was spent in physical therapy sessions, medical testing, rehabilitation activities and, in some cases, absence from or significant change of employment.

I never forget that for each client this is her/his only (hopefully) lawsuit. The only chance at monetary compensation. The only chance at justice.

I know that my courageous clients never wanted to end up in my office. They never wanted to have physical and emotional limitations in their lives. They never wanted to enter forced retirement from work due to a permanent disability. They never wanted to get struck by a car, fall off of a scaffold or encounter a negligent doctor.

No one plans to be injured or killed by negligence or medical malpractice. No one foresees themselves as an innocent victim. No one spends a minute thinking about a circumstance wherein they did nothing wrong, yet their lives changed for the worse in an instant because someone else wasn't paying attention, wasn't living up to standards of their profession or wasn't all that interested in creating a safe environment.

I have spent my entire career having the noble opportunity to represent those who have been victimized and had to face tenacious pushback from the forces of powerful corporations and insurance companies to ensure justice was done no matter the odds.

I thank all of my clients who make my battles on their behalf meaningful, rewarding and always worth fighting with every ounce of my energy. This book is dedicated to each and every one of you whose spirit and valor inspire me daily.

I have spent my entire career having the noble opportunity to represent those who have been victimized and had to face tenacious pushback from the forces of powerful corporations and insurance companies to ensure justice was done no matter the odds.

two
The Insurance Company's Worst Nightmare - **Me**

In virtually every personal injury and medical mal-practice case if any payment of a settlement or judgment is won it will be made by an insurance company. The usual exceptions are cases wherein no insurance is available (rarely do lawyers pursue those cases due to the slim chance of collecting any money); there is a "self-insured" retention which means that the party with insurance pays a portion of the settlement before the insurance money becomes available; or the party is fully self-insured such as a city or other governmental entity.

The insurance companies also hire the attorneys to defend the case. Sometimes the lawyers are in-house firms working exclusively on cases for a particular insurance company and other times private firms are retained by the insurance company on a case-by-case basis. Either way, the insurance company controls the power of the purse and often directs the course of litigation (the process of a lawsuit) ending in either a settlement or a trial.

The Insurance Adjuster

Soon after you are in a car accident, a construction accident or a falldown at a building you will likely receive a phone call or a letter from an insurance adjuster inquiring about your accident. The adjuster may sound friendly, sympathetic and caring. **DO NOT BE FOOLED.**

The insurance adjuster has one goal and one goal only - pay you as little money as possible for the injuries you sustained. That is the plan, plain and simple. The adjuster is not your friend. The adjuster does not care about your recovery. The adjuster is not interested in you receiving fair and just compensation for your pain and suffering, loss of enjoyment of life and lost wages now and into the future.

I am not saying that all or many adjusters are cold and heartless people. Some may be very nice human beings. However, for purposes of their work assignment they are in the business of saving money for their employers. Insurance companies are in the business of collecting premiums from drivers, construction companies, doctors, nursing homes, manufacturers, hospitals, landlords, etc. After collecting those premiums, they seek to invest those moneys and increase their investment portfolios and profits to the maximum degree.

That is their general business model and that is fine for them. Not so fine for you.

You, as a victim of an accident or medical malpractice, stand in the way of them achieving the largest financial growth possible. You, in their eyes, are the claimant who seeks money from them which reduces their profits, reduces their investments and interferes with their tidy business model.

Adjusters are in the business of "risk management". Managing risk means either insuring low risk clients (e.g., the relatively very small number of construction companies and landlords that put safety over profit) or paying out claims in as small amounts as possible for higher risk clients (almost everyone else). Every time substantial payouts are made to victims like you the insurance company is now potentially paying out more in claims than they are taking in for premiums. That is obviously not a profitable business model if they are paying out large numbers on claims and collecting much smaller numbers on premiums. Point made.

Let's take the example of a car accident and the adjuster's contact with you. The adjuster for the insurance company that insures the vehicle that caused your injuries dreams about speaking to you before you hire a lawyer. They will make that friendly first call to you to see how you are feeling. They will express concern. They may even say that their insured (the person responsible for the accident) may share some fault for the accident. They will also ask if it is alright to record the phone conversation with you when asking questions about the accident and your injuries.

You are vulnerable. You are confused. You hopefully have had no past experience as an accident victim. Since the adjuster sounds helpful, you lean toward saying yes and will cooperate with the insurance company. **BIG MISTAKE. Never let an insurance adjuster record a conversation and never give them written statements. Your only response to their calls should be "I will take down your contact information and claim number. I am in the process of hiring a lawyer and my lawyer will contact you directly. Please do not call me again".**

Sounds harsh? Not as harsh as giving away information that will surely be used against you after you go to an attorney and your lawsuit begins. No good (except the good for insurance companies) has ever come from speaking to an insurance adjuster before consulting an attorney. None. Ever.

In your weakest moments, close in time to sustaining serious injuries in an accident, you are being asked to let the insurance company for the person/company at fault to frame questions that may lead to information that can only help them and hurt you. **DON'T DO IT. I'M BEGGING YOU. DON'T DO IT.**

Consult an attorney after a serious accident, medical malpractice event or nursing home incident as soon as you are physically able to. If for no other reason, you want to find out about your rights. **If an attorney accepts your case, the adjuster can no longer ethically contact you directly.** The case will now be fought by an attorney who, if you chose carefully, concentrates in the area of personal injury/medical malpractice and will know how to handle the matter in a manner most advantageous to you.

The Legal Steps

So now, hopefully, you have chosen and retained (signed an agreement for the attorney to represent you) an attorney. The insurance adjuster is out of your hair and her/his last best chance of settling directly with you for pennies on the dollar has flown away. Good for you. Bad for the insurance company.

Once you sign a written retainer with your attorney then legal work begins. First, you will be signing a contingency fee retainer which means that **you pay no fee unless you win.** If you win (by settlement or verdict), the lawyer gets paid a percentage of the settlement (usually 33-1/3% on personal injury cases and a bit less in medical malpractice cases) plus disbursements (expenses such as court filing fees, deposition transcript costs, investigation costs, expert fees, etc.). This arrangement allows people with very limited financial means to get excellent legal representation because there are no upfront legal fees. The only legal fees come at the end of the case and only if you win.

Once you have retained a lawyer, your potential road to a financial recovery begins. I say potential because personal injury/medical malpractice cases do not come with guarantees.* There are many elements that go into a winning case and almost never is a case a slam dunk due to all of these variables.

Step one

Step one is the initial evaluation of the case by your attorney. That evaluation is based upon your version of what happened and how it has physically and emotionally affected you. Clients need to understand that even assuming that everything they tell their lawyer is 100% accurate in their eyes, the parties who allegedly caused the accident and injuries are extremely likely to disagree on many points.

Once you hire a lawyer, the insurance company loses its last best chance at settling the case for pennies on the dollar with an accident victim whose injuries are at an early stage and whose knowledge of fair value is zero. When a lawyer steps in, the adjuster knows the game has changed forever. No more taking advantage of victims who will give statements that they are not required to give. No more victims who may give away the case because she/he does not understand value, especially at an early stage.

---

*   Prior results cannot and do not guarantee a similar outcome.

No more chance at saving the insurance company substantial money by accepting low ball settlements that the victim has no idea are low ball.

Step two

The next thing your attorney will do after being retained is to begin an investigation into the case. Depending on the facts of your case that may mean hiring an investigator,

> Once you hire a lawyer, the insurance company loses its last best chance at settling the case for pennies on the dollar

an engineer or a medical expert or maybe all three. Sometimes these things must be done early in the case, other times they can be done at later stages and sometimes not at all based upon your unique fact pattern. What are the functions of each of these?

Investigation

The necessity and extent of an investigation depends wholly on the facts and circumstances of your accident. A few examples will illustrate this point.

If you are in a car accident as a pedestrian, passenger or driver, there is likely a police report that must be obtained.

Most times **clients are in the best position to obtain copies of police reports quickly.** If circumstances (death or severe disability) do not allow that an investigator hired by your lawyer's office will get the report.

Sometimes, the police report will list witness information. Whether favorable or unfavorable to your case, it is best for the investigator to obtain a signed statement from the witness detailing her/his account of how the accident happened. Your lawyer needs to know early on in the case what a disinterested witness' (one who is not a party and will not benefit from either side succeeding in a lawsuit) version of the accident is in writing. The investigator will attempt to locate the witness and ascertain if the witness is willing to cooperate in giving a statement. There are times when witnesses simply do not want to become involved.

There are times when there are no known witnesses, but the accident happened in a heavily trafficked area or at a large apartment building. Sometimes the investigator is able to canvass the area and ask enough people to be led to a previously unknown witness. I recently had a case at an intersection that was busy at certain hours due to an influx of commercial building tenants at lunchtime. My investigator canvassed the area at the same time of day and same day of the week asking everyone within earshot whether they had witnessed my client's accident the week before. While extremely rare, he hit pay dirt. Someone told him that a friend not only witnessed it but made a video of the scene immediately following the accident which showed the position of the truck and my pedestrian client lying on the pavement next to the truck's wheel. The friend walked my investigator over to the witnesses' apartment building and the result was locating a critical witness (not listed on the police report) and video that was very favorable to our client's case. Hard work by the investigator and some good luck were a potent combination in that instance.

In a car accident scenario, at times the placement of a stop sign, the contours of the roadway or the visibility at an intersection may become at issue. In those instances, an investigator needs to take a series of photographs from multiple perspectives to capture the perspective of the drivers/pedestrian/bicyclist as they existed at the time of the incident. Many times, an investigator's diagrams are helpful for a better understanding of the accident details.

What if you unfortunately fell on a defect on a sidewalk, in a stairwell or in a store? Optimally, you or a companion took a photo of the defect soon after the accident. If you were rushed to the hospital and alone this probably will not happen. Dispatching an investigator to the scene as soon as possible (if the defect is still there and open to the public) is essential. Photos of the actual defect and measurements of the length, width and depth of the defect are extremely useful tools during a trial to allow a jury a full understanding of the dangerous condition that caused your falldown.

In construction accident cases the result is often catastrophic injuries or death. If an investigator cannot get on site to photograph defects, he may be able to speak to one of the victim's friends who are co-workers and instruct them on how to take useful photos of the defect inside an employees-only area of the site.

Investigators do all of the above as well as find parties whose original addresses don't check out or who try to avoid service of legal papers. Hiring an experienced, top notch investigator is an essential part of preparing many personal injury cases.

Engineers/Safety Experts

There are many cases that require the expertise of an engineer, a safety consultant or another type of scientific expert. Hiring the right kind of expert is determined by the particulars of your case. Not every case requires an expert, but any case that requires an expert mandates that the right kind of expert is hired. Such an expert must be as good at her/his science as she/he is at communicating opinions in lay language to jurors. Without the second quality, the first quality is virtually useless at trial.

A simple example is a road design and maintenance case I handled a number of years ago. The unusually low and circular median barrier in Brooklyn dividing oncoming traffic acted as a catapult. I hired a traffic design engineer with superb credentials to go out to the roadway and carefully examine the barrier in addition to taking pictures and reviewing documents and data. As good as his educational and professional background was, it turned out to be his trial testimony presentation manner that won over the jury. He constructed a re-creation of the scene from his inspection and police photos. He had small toy cars which he used to demonstrate the accident (this was pre-internet, but I think its simplicity would still be effective today). An expert's calculations, reconstruction and scientific foundations are necessary in such a case, but her/his ability to communicate and relate to everyday jurors was key. Remember back to your school days. If the teacher or professor was a genius but could not make the subject matter easily understandable to her/his students, then she/he failed as a teacher. Jurors are the equivalent of students. If they do not understand the explanations they will likely not be persuaded by the presenter (your expert witness).

I have had cases where there are sharp disputes in testimony as to how an accident happened. The client has one version, the party being sued has another version and an eyewitness has a third version. If there is enough data (photos, measurements, skid marks, placement of vehicles, etc.), I have had biomechanical engineers examine the site, review the testimony and study available documents and photos. From their review, they have been able to make an engineering reconstruction of how the accident happened, the speed of the vehicles and the forces involved in the crash. While no reconstruction is 100% accurate (the other side often hires their own biomechanical engineer to dispute our engineer's findings), it acts as a guide for jurors who are being asked to choose between different human memories of the accident. Any time I can help a jury find the correct path to my client's position through a scientific approach I am all in.

What about using an expert for a slip and fall on ice accident on subway steps? Does that require an expert? Normally I would say no, but I had a case recently that was unusual enough that I hired an engineer to evaluate the facts and testify at trial. My engineer found that the subway steps were under renovation and there was space created by the construction between the edge of the steps and the wall. The space did not have proper drainage so when snow was shoveled into the space area, it would melt when temperatures rose or ice melt was applied. The problem, he determined, was that the temporary melting led to re-formed ice on the subway steps after the temperature precipitously dropped. The refreezing could have been avoided with more vigilant inspection of the steps, the use of more ice melt, more frequent inspections and more diligent snow removal from the empty space area.

> Any time I can help a jury find the correct path to my client's position through a scientific approach I am all in.

As knowledgeable as my engineer was, it was his simple description to the jury that helped us win the case. On direct examination at trial, I had him explain every scientific and engineering terms in simple and understandable language. Jurors are composed of people whose educational levels range from 8th grade and high school to degrees from law school, medical school and Ph.D. programs. All jurors must understand each witness' testimony. Every jurors' vote is equal. No technical or scientific background of jurors is assumed. Having the ability to speak on everyone's level, regardless of educational or employment background is a vital skill for experts in a courtroom. Choosing the right expert is essential if the case goes to trial. As a precaution, I always assume every case goes to trial so I am never caught without all of the right kinds of witnesses I need to be in the best position possible to succeed at trial.

Ever hear of a materials' science expert? I now know about this field from one of my cases. My client was using a piece of elastic gym equipment when he stretched it out and it literally broke and a piece struck him in the face at great velocity. We got the actual piece of equipment since his friend recovered it from the garbage where the gym employees threw it out after the accident. I hired a materials' science expert who examined and tested it in his lab to determine if the fibers broke from wear and tear or from a product defect. The scientist bought a new version of the same product to compare how much use it would take to get to the point of breaking. He showed me through a microscope how the fibers looked at different stages of use. The scientist determined that the product itself was not defective but there was negligent maintenance of the equipment by the gym in allowing the elastic band to remain in such frail condition and still be available for use by unsuspecting gym patrons.

I once hired a safety consultant on a case involving a recessed floor drain that caused an industrial food cart to topple over and spill piping hot food onto my client's upper body. Her burns required a month's hospitalization in a burn center and left her with significant and permanent scars. To a lay person's eye, a drain inches below floor level catching a cart tire may seem obvious, but there was more to the analysis than one would think. There are accepted industry standards regarding pushing vs. pulling when operating a food cart. There are accepted industry standards as to how a floor drain should be constructed in an industrial kitchen as to both maximize drainage and ensure worker safety. The safety consultant identified many issues that would not be apparent to the average eye.

At trial, the other side (12 parties on the other side in total) presented their own contrary expert testimony on these issues. While the qualifications of my expert and the opposing experts were virtually equal, my safety engineer presented the issues in such a way to the jury that seemed credible and relatable. Instead of using engineering words that were technical and scientific, his discussion was understandable and incorporated simple explanations and common examples to illustrate his points. Once again, the great teachers don't just master the material, they get their students (in this case, jurors) to master the material through interesting, informative and entertaining presentations.

I once had a case involving a Manhattan sidewalk grate that was partially bent which caused my client to trip, fall and sustain life-altering injuries. My safety expert, after he inspected the grate, concluded this bending shape exhibited in a few slats was not simple wear and tear. It was clearly done by mechanical tools (likely a screwdriver) that the maintenance personnel of the adjoining office building used to remove cigarette butts that were lodged between the slats. Instead of screwing off the grates and cleaning the cigarette butts out properly, the maintenance workers took the easy and dangerous way out resulting in bent slats - bent enough for one's shoe to get caught in the open space. My expert's theory was one that the other side never thought of, but it resulted in a winning argument that led to a very substantial settlement on the eve of trial.

You may be wondering how my engineering and safety experts get to examine these defective conditions when they exist in non-public areas such as inside buildings or within construction sites. That's where I come in. Depending on the point at which my client retains me (getting to a lawyer early always is to your advantage), I go to court to obtain a court order either before suit is commenced or after suit is started to have my expert go to the scene in the presence of me (I like to personally observe the condition since I will have the job of explaining it to jurors at trial before and after my expert takes the stand in opening statements and summation), my client (if physically able to be there) and the other side's attorneys. Under these controlled circumstances, my expert gets adequate time to inspect and conduct non-destructive testing at the accident scene. Of course, if my client has access to the accident scene (her/his apartment for example) or it is on a public sidewalk or stairwell the inspection can be done as early as possible by our expert without a court order.

If a client comes to me at a later stage, the condition of the scene may have changed to a degree that an inspection is useless. The best we can do at that point is to reconstruct the scene through testimony, documents and pre-accident pictures if any exist. **This is another good reason why contacting a lawyer as soon as possible after an accident gives you an advantage in succeeding in your lawsuit.**

Medical Experts

Often times you treat for injuries with very fine doctors and surgeons. They are highly qualified. They practice at world-class hospitals. They use state of the art medical techniques. They comfort you and give you confidence. All of that is what you should look for in a treating physician.

Unfortunately, in the legal arena while those traits are all admirable, they are not enough to impress jurors and insurance companies. Quite often, the esteemed treating orthopedic surgeon, neurosurgeon or plastic surgeon has absolutely no interest in becoming involved in your lawsuit. She/he will cooperate, as required by law with your consent, to the extent of sending your lawyer and the other side's lawyer medical records but that is it. They refuse to write narrative reports detailing their visits with you, their findings, their surgeries, their diagnosis and their future prognosis (forecasts for future medical issues resulting from your injuries). They detest coming to court and having their opinions and treatment choices questioned by the defense lawyers on cross-examination. They do not know how to establish a rapport with jurors. They speak in medical terms without lay explanations. Simply, other than their treatment records they are of no help in your case.

There are rare exceptions, but most treating physicians/surgeons are not helpful in structuring narrative reports into cohesive language and are even less helpful at testifying in court. In those instances, your lawyer needs to know highly qualified doctors and surgeons who understand the field of forensic medicine, i.e., applying medical knowledge to analyze facts in your case on the issues of causation (whether your injuries were caused by your accident) and permanency (whether your injuries have left you with effects for the rest of your life). There is an art and science to forensic medicine. The kinds of medical experts that I choose when necessary in personal injury cases understand that certain issues must be addressed in a narrative report that will be read by defense lawyers, insurance adjusters and judges. The contents will be subject to a rigorous cross examination at trial so the essential exam testing, categories of findings and breadth of opinions are critical elements in preparation of a medical report used in a legal case. While both your treating physician/surgeon and the examining medical expert chosen by your lawyer are both certainly telling the truth, usually only the forensic expert knows the nuance of which medico-legal terms must be used and which areas must be addressed in a comprehensive narrative report which will be used both in settlement discussions and as the basis for direct examination (by your lawyer) and cross-examination (by the opposing lawyer) at trial. While absolute honesty is the foundation of every narrative report, knowing how to formulate and present the report in a proper format is a necessity for any physician or surgeon writing one in your case.

So, what if your case does not settle? Will the chosen expert doctor/surgeon come to trial? Yes. That is the whole point. While these expert forensic doctors almost always still have active medical/surgical practices, they understand that their presence at trial is mandatory if your case goes to trial. Not only must they make time to have a trial prep session with your lawyer, they must also move their schedules around to accommodate the judge's trial schedule if necessary.

What is the value of having an expert medical witness testify on your behalf when your treating physician/surgeon refuses to come to court and is simply fearful about testifying because she/he just isn't comfortable doing that? The value is immeasurable.

Firstly, a seasoned expert understands his role before a jury. She/he is a teacher not an advocate. You have a lawyer as your advocate. Your medical expert is the authority who educates the jury about your injuries, your surgeries, your permanent pain and suffering and limitations. Remember when I discussed engineering experts earlier? The same goes for medical experts. They must know how to connect with average jurors. The average juror did not go to medical school. The average juror did not take a course in anatomy. The average juror did not have plates, rods, pins or screws inserted in her/his leg. The average juror does not know the meaning of "total knee replacement", "artificial hip" or "traumatic arthritis". The best forensic medical experts know how to bring these terms to life in simple and everyday terms. They know how to demonstrate their specialized knowledge using illustrative graphics or anatomical models. They know how to bring dull x-ray films or MRI films to life. They know that their audience is not a group of medical students.

The best experts spend direct examination (when your lawyer questions them) being your favorite high school teacher or college professor. They know the best way to impart knowledge with an entertaining style. They know when to inject appropriate humor even in the most serious cases. They know that jurors are judging their honesty, integrity and credibility the whole time they are on the witness stand. They do not shy away from eye contact with the jurors. They initiate eye contact with the jurors. They are as comfortable on that witness stand as they are in their own offices with their patients. Public speaking is a gift and the really good ones have it.

As important as direct examination is by your lawyer, cross examination by the opposing lawyer is critical. If the other lawyer catches your witness in falsehoods, inconsistencies or unsupported opinions, every good thing that happened during direct examination may be erased. This is why the selection of a seasoned forensic medical expert is essential in many cases.

The doctor who is comfortable in the courtroom understands his role during cross examination. She/he doesn't get flustered. She/he concedes points when they are objectively correct (**Q.**– The plaintiff made no neck complaints at the emergency room? **A.**–Correct.). If that is what the emergency room record shows it is indisputable. She/he never fights or talks back disrespectfully to the cross-examiner during questioning. She/he answers questions calmly because she/he is a woman/man of science. She/he remembers she/he is not an advocate, but a teacher. She/he is prepared for questions about her/his prior cases that she/he has testified in if her/his conclusions in your case are different (all cases are fact specific and unique so there are no one-size-fits-all answers). She/he knows that sarcastic responses and an arrogant demeanor toward the opposing attorney are absolutely destructive to the medical expert's credibility in the courtroom. The confident teacher knows that her/his job is to teach and it is the lawyer's job to directly persuade the jurors by framing the evidence during opening, direct, cross examination and summation. The great teacher indirectly persuades the jurors by simply being honest, open, informative, entertaining (not with song and dance, but simply by being human and personable) and relatable. Many a case with injuries in dispute has been won, in part, by effective medical testimony at trial by the injured party's medical expert.

It should be noted that unlike the engineering or safety experts, medical experts are usually not chosen until a later stage of the case. Once all of the medical treatment is essentially completed and it is determined that the treating physician/surgeon either will not or should not testify (due to inexperience in lawsuits, fear of the courtroom or unavailability), then the medical expert will be retained by your lawyer to examine you, write a narrative report and be prepared to testify at trial. The exception is in medical malpractice and nursing home cases.

When I do the initial intake on medical malpractice and nursing home cases, I make it clear to clients that no final decision on whether there is a viable lawsuit (not a guaranteed winner but a suit with merit) can be made until after medical records are obtained and a medical review is completed. Once I receive the pertinent medical records, I send them to a physician for review as to the potential acts of medical or nursing home negligence. In my discussion with the expert, I let her/

him know the legal standards for malpractice or negligence. A simple act of bad judgment is not the test. In New York, the doctor must fail to meet the generally accepted standard of care before malpractice can be proven. That is a very high standard. Even if this breach of the standard of care can be established by a preponderance of the evidence (tipping of the scales of justice just over the 50% mark), there still has to be adequate proof that the malpractice or negligence caused the injury or death.

Therefore, very early in the process I have a detailed discussion with an expert physician whether or not there is a good faith basis to bring a case. I have great confidence in my experts since they give objective, honest and reasoned opinions without an agenda. The good expert does not come in with a rooting interest. The good experts are like the good umpires. She/he only cares about the facts and the scientific basis for opinions. They call them as they see them.

There is no greater disservice a lawyer can do to a potential medical malpractice/nursing home negligence client than to view the case through rose-colored glasses at the inception. Your lawyer should not be a mindless cheerleader for your case. He/she should be a zealous advocate for you only if your case has merit. If not, the lawyer should reject you case. When I say merit, I mean that the case has a reasonable expectation of succeeding at trial. There are never guarantees that your case will result in a win. That would be a misleading promise.

Your lawyer can only promise an earnest, zealous and professional effort to put your case in the most favorable light as possible in the eyes of insurance companies, judges and jurors. That promise is contingent on an early and objective analysis by your attorney which continues throughout your case as more records, testimony and facts are revealed. Many cases are like roller coasters. They rise up, they dip down and the cycle starts all over again.

Starting Suit

After I do a client interview and obtain a signed retainer agreement (a contingency fee means that no attorney fee is charged that no attorney fee is charged unless the case is successful and the fee then comes out of your share of the award only if you win), my work on a client's behalf begins. You are now familiar with my reliance on investigators, engineers, safety consultants and medical experts. All of the above are done in conjunction with sending for medical records, doing property searches and collecting publicly available relevant documents. The next phase is a legal analysis of those documents and items.

I have great confidence in my experts since they give objective, honest and reasoned opinions without an agenda.

Once I have your version of the accident or malpractice, documentation of the injuries and other information (e.g. witness statements, expert opinions if necessary, etc.), I can make the final decision whether your case merits starting a lawsuit. I use my experience and expertise to analyze the unique facts of your case and the applicable law of New York. All of the above is not a quick process. Investigation takes time. Obtaining medical records takes time. Expert inspections and analysis take time. You want your lawyer to get it right, not get it quickly at the risk of missing vital pieces.

Once I have determined that my client's claim has merit, I must determine who are the proper parties to sue. This process may include reviewing police reports, fire department records, medical records, witness statements, property searches or more documents. All of this analysis must be done within the time limit to sue (known as the statute of limitations). In some cases against municipalities the time to make the initial claim (known as a notice of claim which is filed pre-suit) may be as little as a number of months so many times this notice is made based upon your version of events and little else so as to preserve your right to sue. General negligence cases, medical malpractice cases and wrongful death cases against private persons and entities, with exceptions, may have multi-year statutes to start lawsuits but one never wants to wait until the statute is about to expire.

Once the decision is made that your case has merit (merit does not mean you are guaranteed to win, it means that there is enough reasonable evidence to go forward), I prepare a summons and complaint. The summons is simply written notification to the defendants (the parties being sued) of my client's lawsuit and the complaint is the accompanying document that sets out in usually bare (not detailed at this point) legal language the allegations of when and where the incident happened and that the defendants were negligent and the cause of plaintiff's (you, the client, are the plaintiff) injuries or death.

The summons and complaint are filed with the clerk in the county where the lawsuit is brought. The particular county in a New York court action is chosen by the plaintiff and generally must be either where the plaintiff or defendant resided at the time suit began or the location of accident (with some exceptions).

After the filing of the summons and complaint, I hire a process serving firm to serve the summons and complaint on the defendants either personally or by other legally acceptable means. When the insurance company gets wind that a party insured by it has been served, it knows the battle has begun and the behemoth insurance company now knows it is up against a knowledgeable lawyer for the rest of the fight. **THIS IS WHY INSURANCE COMPANIES HATE WHEN YOU HIRE A LAWYER. YOU LEVEL THE PLAYING FIELD.**

Once the insurance company is notified by the person or company served with the summons and complaint, it is the duty of the insurance company to hire lawyers (part of your average insurance policy is the obligation of the insurance company to hire and pay for lawyers on your behalf when you are the defendant - the one being sued). I usually hear from the insurance company directly that they received the summons and complaint and are in the process of hiring attorneys. Sometimes the law firm itself notifies me in the first instance.

The next step is for the defendants' (remember, that's the term for the parties you are suing) attorney(s) to respond with a legal "Answer". The answer is a very bare document denying most of the allegations in the complaint and denying enough present knowledge to admit or deny other allegations (translation - the lawyers haven't yet interviewed their clients to prepare definitive responses to your claims). Along with the answer comes a package of legal demands for relevant documents and authorizations from you for your medical and lost wages records which your lawyer must supply the defense with as a matter of law.

Your lawyer will then also send out a demand to the defense lawyer for relevant documents as well. The next phase varies by county in New York (all references to New York court actions mean state court, not federal court). In some counties a preliminary conference is scheduled by the court wherein the plaintiff's and defendants' attorneys appear to fill out a document that the court orders with respect to documents and information that must be provided by both sides. In other counties, the court fills out the order without the attorneys present. The order also sets down dates for examinations before trial (a/k/a depositions - sworn oral testimony by the parties about the facts of the accident and the resultant injuries). It sets a time schedule for you to undergo physical examinations by defendants' doctors (more about this in the next chapter). It also sets up a court date for the parties to appear in court to advise the judge about the progress of discovery (a legal term for the exchange of documents, examinations before trial and physical exams by defendants). This court date is known as a compliance conference.

The exchange of documents that takes place next can be very enlightening at times. If you weren't honest with your lawyer about never speaking to the insurance company or its investigators before contacting him/her, now is the time you will be found out. If you gave the insurance company a recorded statement or a written statement it will now be served on your attorney. It is never good news when I receive such a statement since the previously unrepresented client almost always agrees to whatever words the adjuster or investigator suggests about the accident and injuries. **Remember when I told you earlier that the adjuster may be friendly but isn't your friend?** These statements usually bear out that truism. Hopefully, whatever you said to the adjuster isn't fatal to your case but now is the time I need to confront the client as to what he/she meant when giving the statement. The statement may misrepresent what you said but a juror may not see it your way. You said it, read it and maybe signed it so jurors usually believe you own it. I will deal with this part of your case as I deal with all other elements. I will argue to a jury by putting your statement in the best, most honest and logical light possible. **LET THIS SERVE AS FURTHER PROOF WHY YOU**

SHOULD HIRE A LAWYER BEFORE SPEAKING TO AN INSURANCE ADJUSTER.

After reviewing the information sent by the defendants and analyzing the documents I received from my investigator or experts, it is time to meet you to discuss your examination before trial (the opposing lawyer will ask you questions about the incident and injuries and you will answer under oath) in your lawyer's presence. Many times, these examinations before trial get adjourned for a variety of viable reasons so this meeting may not take place for quite some time. Close to the time of the testimony, I meet with the client to set the rules of engagement. Postponements (adjournments) of your testimony are common and will not be confirmed until the day before your examination before trial. **BE PATIENT.** Postponements are beyond your lawyer's control. The next chapter will elaborate on this preparation (prep) session.

Once your examination before trial is done, the examinations before trial of the defendants will take place. The time frame for this to happen varies by the case so it could be days, weeks, months or even years later. This is my opportunity to question the defendants about their versions of the incident. Rarely is there an admission of fault, but at least I can learn what their defenses are going to be and now they are locked into sworn testimony about the events that caused the accident.

By the end of the defendants' examinations before trial, the factual disputes between the parties become clearer. The legal issues now begin to crystallize since the facts dictate how the law is applied (legal speak for getting to the point where the law that applies to your case becomes clearer after the testimony is in). Additional document requests may be made. Also, motions (applications to the court to force the other side to provide certain information not previously disclosed) may be made by either side. Sometimes resolution of these motions takes many months and may require a court appearance. The delay is just another factor that makes the slow process of a lawsuit even slower.

The plaintiff (you again) will also have to submit to a physical exam by doctor(s) of defendants' choosing and that physician(s) will render a report with examination findings, opinions on causation, diagnosis and prognosis. Almost never are these reports supportive of the plaintiff's position. These reports will also be the basis for the defendants' doctors' testimony at trial if the case reaches that stage.

While I zipped through the process of my legal work to this point, it must be remembered that a lawyer's time spent on your case usually consists of many, many long hours. Personal injury/medical malpractice lawyers representing plaintiffs work on a contingency fee, so you never get billed for hours. Rest assured that any good plaintiffs' lawyer spends countless hours on legal research, preparation, court appearances, drafting and reviewing documents, conducting and defending examinations before trial and constant analysis of every aspect of your case. I haven't even discussed the massive hours that go into preparing, arguing and opposing critical motions (legal applications to the judge), conducting discovery (the pre-trial work I discussed already), attending settlement conferences/mediations, preparing for trial and actually trying the case.

A good lawyer's work is constant, intense and fluid (facts, legal rulings and scheduling all change on a dime during the long course of a case). Choosing an experienced, knowledgeable and dedicated attorney for your personal injury or medical malpractice case is extremely important. Your case must be prepared and presented in a persuasive, professional and understandable manner at every stage. The insurance adjuster, the defense counsel, the judge and the jury know the difference between lawyers who put in the homework, have the experience and exhibit keen legal minds and those that don't. Choose wisely when retaining

Choosing an experienced, knowledgeable and dedicated attorney for your personal injury or medical malpractice case is extremely important. Your case must be prepared and presented in a persuasive, professional and understandable manner at every stage.

an attorney. It may make a very significant difference in how your case proceeds and resolves.*

No reputable lawyer guarantees future results. Decisions about which lawyer to choose and why are solely for each client to make. When early promises are made to you by your lawyer about how your case will resolve, beware. No lawyer can promise a result.* Ask your questions, be informed and be sure you feel confident that your attorney will fight for your rights at every stage of your case.

Settlement/Mediation

Now we get close to the final phase of your case. The discovery is done. The court is informed in writing that the case is ready for trial and no party objects to that statement. This is the beginning of the end game for your case.

In some, but not many, of my substantial cases there are settlement discussions before the case is placed on the court's trial calendar (the point where all discovery is done). An adjuster may see the handwriting on the wall and want to settle the case without the additional time and legal expenses of pre-trial dispositive motions (those applications in which a judge can determine which side is at fault as a matter of law or those in which injuries do not meet a legal threshold which is applicable in motor vehicle cases only), pre-trial court conferences,

---

*   Prior results cannot and do not guarantee a similar outcome.

trial preparation, trial and potential appeals. Settlement discussions are always welcome at any stage, but a client should never have an expectation that a settlement can be concluded at a relatively early stage (before the case is placed on the trial calendar). No one knows which cases may settle early, which ones may never settle (i.e., a jury verdict concludes the case) and which may be appealed even after a jury verdict (another long delay in the process of resolving your case, if necessary).

Assuming yours is the normal case that does not settle by the end of discovery, in New York court cases require filing a note of issue (informing the court and opposing counsel that the case is ready for trial) which begins the clock ticking on scheduling a trial date. The wait time is not only specific to each county in New York, it is forever changing within counties based on court backlogs, new directives by court administrators and so many other factors that I won't go into since it will make your head spin and probably change by the time you finish this book.

Suffice to say, once your case is on the court's trial calendar in the New York state court system, you are generally closer to the end of your case then the beginning ("end" is a relative term because trial scheduling time frames are forever changing in New York). Now is the time for dispositive (those that may end a case) motions which I will explain below.

A dispositive motion is essentially an application to a judge by a party to dismiss the other party's case on specific legal grounds. If the judge grants the motion the case may be over (or maybe not, if only parts of the motion are granted) or may become the subject of an appeal if such legal grounds for an appeal exist.

The parties have specific time limits after the case is first placed on the court calendar to make these dispositive motions, also known as summary judgment motions. Not all fact patterns lend themselves to such motions, but they are more often made in construction cases, automobile cases and falldown cases due to long-standing (and often changing) laws and legal precedents. These motions tend to be very complicated, require lots of legal research and may end your case without a jury ever hearing a word of testimony. There are so many different legal issues involved in the body of cases that are ripe for summary judgment that it would not be helpful to readers to learn about them here. Most importantly, you need to be aware that your case may have the potential to be dismissed by a judge before trial. Your lawyer can advise as to his/her thoughts on the merits of a summary judgment motion under the particular facts of your case, but no one ever can predict how a particular judge will rule on any specific case. By now, I think you have gotten the hint that lawsuits are not fertile ground for predictions and guarantees. **Simply, any lawyer that makes guarantees or makes promises to you about the results of your lawsuit is doing you a disservice.** I can't predict the results of football games, elections, lawsuits and a host of other events. No one can. **Run, don't walk, out**

of a lawyer's office if she/he tells you your case is a slam dunk. Slam dunks only exist in basketball, not lawsuits.

In most cases there are no summary judgment motions (applications by either side to the judge to dismiss the case before a jury trial) and the case sits on the court trial calendar awaiting pre-trial settlement conferences. Many times, the conferences are not fruitful because the case has not been timely evaluated by the insurance adjuster or the adjuster does not share your attorney's view of the value of the case. You must understand that every personal injury/medical malpractice lawsuit is evaluated on a case-by-case basis. No magic settlement number exists based on past cases, your friend's "similar case" or your cousin's view of the case. The value of your case is based on so many different factors ranging from how different the versions of the accident are as evidenced by the testimony of each party; how your injuries have continued to affect you; how much lost earnings you can prove; how much conflict there will be in engineering, medical or other expert testimony on each side; the kind of jury that will hear your case; the judge's evidentiary rulings in your case at trial and so many more tangible and intangible factors.

> Run, don't walk, out of a lawyer's office if she/he tells you your case is a slam dunk. Slam dunks only exist in basketball, not lawsuits.

Of course, if the insurance coverage on the other side is limited that becomes a critical aspect of the case. Recovering a judgment beyond insurance policy limits is almost always unrealistic so insurance policy limits essentially set the ceiling for your financial recovery. However, never focus on how large an insurance policy is in your case. Just because the limits of the policy are a million dollars does not in any way, shape or form determine that is the value of your case. The value of your case, as previously stated, is shaped by innumerable factors. A large insurance policy is not a factor unless your case has outstanding liability (fault) in your favor and the damages are truly catastrophic. No insurance company ever gives away money just because it has a large policy. The value of a case is whatever number is agreed upon by the parties within the limits of the insurance policy. The amount of the policy is only relevant when the policy is limited (For example, New York has a $25,000 minimum generally for not-for-hire automobile policies). Large policies only mean large recoveries when the case merits such a number. It is a difficult concept to explain to my clients, but it is reality. Remember, insurance companies are in business to take in premiums and pay as little on claims as possible. They do not give away large sums of money in lawsuits unless they believe there is a high risk that a jury will award a large sum of money. **THAT IS WHY INSURANCE COMPANIES HATE WHEN YOU HIRE A LAWYER.** Lawyers are there to maximize your recovery by fighting and protecting your legal rights at every stage. Having a lawyer present your case in the most favorable light possible through thorough investigation, intense and focused legal work, experienced analysis and skilled lawyering at every stage is the very thing that insurance companies want to avoid. It is the very reason they try to contact you very early before you retain a lawyer and offer you a settlement figure that you have no way of knowing is fair and just. **INSURANCE COMPANIES DREAD THAT YOU READ THIS BOOK.**

So, assuming your case is sitting on the trial calendar, you survive a summary judgment motion if one is made and court settlement conferences go nowhere, does that mean that the case will go to a jury trial? The short answer is maybe.

Some insurance companies like to have formal settlement discussions on the phone with your attorney during the time your case sits on the court calendar. At times, these discussions are productive and your attorney will keep you advised of formal settlement offers and render advice to you about what he/she feels is a fair and adequate settlement weighed against the risks of letting a jury decide your fate. Depending on the insurance company, the adjuster and how your case unfolded in discovery against the backdrop of legal issues that will undoubtedly come up at trial, your case may be able to get settled by your attorney during phone conferences with the adjuster now that most of the mysteries of the case have been revealed (the biggest mystery to both sides is what a jury of your peers will think of the testimony at trial which is a topic that I will discuss later).

Some insurance companies treat this pre-trial stage as an opportunity to have the case submitted to private mediation (private companies that conduct settlement negotiations with both sides). In the past 25 years, private mediation has become a fixture for some insurance companies to get cases settled before trial. The insurance company can agree to a mediation (initiated by either party) with one of the numerous private mediation companies in New York. These private companies hire lawyers and former judges who have extensive experience either in the private sector or the court system in dealing with settlement negotiations involving personal injury/medical malpractice cases. The participating attorneys for the plaintiff and defendants jointly choose from a roster of mediators (the attorney or ex-judge who conducts the negotiations does so at the mediation company's offices in Manhattan or Long Island for New York City cases). In my experience, I either know the mediators from past mediations (meaning I know when to say yea or nay when choosing a mediator based on my prior impressions) or know of their reputations and methods from a host of colleagues after 37 years of practicing law in New York City. Most mediators are objective, fair and highly skilled in settlement negotiation tactics. The ones that both sides use over and over again are chosen because we all know they are neutral, fair and good at getting two divergent sides to bridge the gap and come to a fair settlement under the circumstances of the particular case.

Once the mediation is scheduled I insist on my client being present. I conduct the negotiations with the mediator but the client is there in a separate room so I can speak to her/him in person at critical stages of the process since the final settlement decision lies with the client after I give my professional advice. Also, if a settlement is reached, I want the client to be there to sign onto the agreement with the understanding that the settlement is voluntary, final and forever.

The client is not in the mediation room since the process is conducted with lawyers, sometimes insurance adjusters and the mediator only. Usually, the process begins with the mediator, the lawyers and insurance adjuster addressing each other with opening remarks about the case. Then the mediator puts the lawyers in separate rooms while shuttling back and forth between the 2 rooms to move the settlement discussions along without each side posturing in front of the other. Confidential conversations with the mediator are a very productive way of moving the discussion forward without making any concessions directly to the other side. I have had mediations last 2 hours, 4 hours, 9 hours and multiple days. Many have resulted in settlements and others have not succeeded. All were worthwhile since they opened up dialogue that previously had been at a stalemate.

The client's presence has other added benefits. The insurance company knows our side is serious about negotiating when the client is out in the waiting room or holding area. The mediator also knows that the client is physically there to sign off on any settlement agreement which is a sign that we came with serious intentions.

A successful mediation happens because both sides understand the strengths and weaknesses of their cases. If your lawyer doesn't put a mirror up to your case, you are not being served well. It is unproductive to view your case only through the eyes of your favorable testimony and ignore the other side's arguments which are often valid. Ignore the weaknesses of your case (every case has weaknesses if you look hard enough) and rest assured whatever those weaknesses are they will be exploited by defense counsel and hammered home again and again to a jury. Remember, jurors come in (hopefully) with open minds. They don't favor a plaintiff before they hear your case and they don't favor defendants before they hear their case. They favor what they find to be the truth when all the testimony and evidence is in at trial. They may agree with you or disagree with you but ignoring that there are at least two possibilities that exist (they could also partially agree with both sides) is a foolish way to think going into a jury trial. Both sides have risks and that is why more cases than not eventually settle to avoid being on the wrong side of the risk when the jury renders its verdict.

Pre-trial Prep

Whether there are ongoing settlement discussions or an upcoming mediation, once your case is on the trial calendar it is progressing toward a trial date. I prepare every case at each stage with the expectation that there will be a jury trial. This ensures that the pre-trial work is done timely and with proper focus. It also sends a message to the defense attorney and insurance adjuster that I am actually ready to try your case if a settlement cannot be reached.

Many, many hours are spent by experienced trial lawyers in pre-trial preparation in the months before a scheduled trial date (never count on a particular date as actually being final since courts are notorious for adjourning trial dates in New York often for reasons known and unknown). These preparations for trial are critically important since the actual trial is the culmination of all the work your lawyer has put in during the years leading up to the trial.

I have always viewed my work as a trial attorney as akin to a boxer. The great boxing champions put in the difficult and long hours of training work far away from the cameras long before a fight. They wake up at 4:00 a.m. to run. They spar for hours with tough sparring partners. They spend countless hours pounding the heavy bag and the speed bag. They have no crowds, no fans, no media watching their tedious, disciplined and laser focused preparation and training. Without these countless hours in the gym and on the jogging trails, their performance in the ring on fight night would never be worthy of a champion.

The trial lawyer's equivalent preparation comes in the form of mental and intellectual skills, but the hours involved are quite similar. Your lawyer, with the herculean efforts of a gifted and relentless assistant (I will match my paralegal Liz against any paralegal in the field. She is incredible. If you are my client, you know what I'm talking about.), needs to prepare for countless hours before your case is ready for the main event, the jury trial.

I have always viewed my work as a trial attorney as akin to a boxer. The great boxing champions put in the difficult and long hours of training work far away from the cameras long before a fight.

Subpoenae (legal papers that order a witness to appear or documents to be produced at trial) must be prepared and served on parties or witnesses that your lawyer seeks to call at trial. Decisions have to be made on which witnesses to call or not. A lot of thought goes into this because having a consistent trial strategy of how to present a case is critical to presenting the best case possible.

Certain hospital records also have to be subpoenaed to ensure their admissibility at trial. Doctor's offices must be

contacted to produce records as well. Very detailed legal procedures must be followed to the letter to make sure they can get into evidence at trial. When I talk about "admissibility" of evidence at trial, I mean it is not good enough to have important documents and records in hand, but it is mandatory that the documents contain the proper certifications and are properly authenticated.

Sometimes, films such as x-rays and MRIs are important pieces of evidence that the testifying doctor needs to support her/his opinions during trial testimony. There are also precise legal rules that must be followed pre-trial to make sure the judge allows them into evidence (i.e., allows the jury to see them and the doctor to refer to them on the witness stand).

Scheduling is one of the most difficult tasks in pre-trial preparation. Witnesses' schedules, doctors' schedules and engineers' schedules do not always coincide with the judge's schedule. Also, the assignment of the judge for trial comes so late in the process (usually after jury selection) that scheduling witnesses by necessity changes from day to day and even hour to hour.

Sometimes, anatomical models or graphics are used by expert witnesses as aids to visually demonstrate points for jurors. Those types of demonstrative exhibits don't just appear at trial. Some can be rented, some need to be purchased and some are so unique that they need to be designed and produced for one-time use. All of this takes time. I can't wait until the eve of trial to think about the exhibits I need at trial. Making decisions about which demonstrative models or graphics to use is a time-consuming process. Ordering them for timely use from the right companies is critically important in particular cases. None of this should be a last-minute exercise.

What about prep sessions? I don't put clients, doctors or engineers/safety experts on the witness stand without meeting with them for a prep session. This consists of me asking them questions that I will pose to them on the witness stand - direct examination. I also need to pepper them with some typical questions that they will get on cross-examination when the opposing attorney attempts to knock them off stride and contradict the testimony just given on direct exam. Cross-examination is an art form and witnesses not used to having words put in their mouth by an opposing lawyer (translation- every witness) need to be taught how to handle the onslaught. The other lawyer's technique may be subtle, but it can be devastating to your case if you or a witness on your behalf sounds like she/he is inconsistent, unsure or not credible.

I haven't even mentioned the legal research and file digesting work that I need to do before every trial which is very time consuming, very detailed and very intense. I literally need to re-review every piece of paper in your file(s). In certain complex cases involving construction accidents, medical malpractice, nursing home negligence and defective products, I may have accumulated 15-25 file folders of documents, legal materials and transcripts during the course of the years from intake through trial. Now every piece of the file must be reorganized into trial folders that follow my anticipated order of testimony and presentation. Not only do I review every piece of paper exchanged in discovery, but I digest deposition transcripts (the written transcripts produced when sworn examination before trial testimony is finished) and voluminous records such as medical records and engineering plans. I need to be thoroughly organized when I need a particular page at my fingertips at a moment's notice during trial. Like the boxer, my audience (the jury) never sees any of these months of preparation. The jury only sees the result which hopefully looks seamless in the courtroom.

How about legal research and legal memos? Every case presents both expected and unexpected legal issues. Judges make decisions on the spot when objections are made or minutes before a witness takes the stand. To make sure the judge is informed, I do extensive legal research on complex issues that I anticipate may arise during trial. I then prepare legal memoranda to hand to the judge to support my argument when the issue does in fact arise. I may begin a trial with 10 of my personally prepared legal memos in my file and end up using none or one. That's fine. A good trial lawyer can never be too prepared. No one can anticipate every legal issue that may pop up at trial but preparing for every issue that I foresee is a critical part of my trial preparation.

At some trials, I know before the trial begins that there will be a particular controversial issue. Maybe I want to prevent the defendants' expert from testifying based on the specific facts and law in my case. Before the trial begins, I will raise the issue and present the judge with a legal memo and argue the merits of my position.

Recently, I did that and persuaded the judge to hold a hearing out of the presence of the jury to determine whether defendants' expert engineer could present opinions before the jury that I argued were "junk science" (alleged "science" not generally accepted in the scientific community). The judge granted my oral motion and the witness took the stand on two separate days (out of the presence of the jury) and was questioned by me, the defendants' attorney and the judge. My preparation paid off and the judge severely limited the nature of the opinion testimony the engineer could give before the jury. This was a rare decision at the time and it proved to be very helpful to my client's case which resulted in a very substantial jury verdict.

If you're not exhausted yet from reading about what goes into my clients' trials, I need to mention a particularly difficult aspect of my pre-trial work - testimony preparation. I go witness by witness preparing each question that I will be asking on direct examination (I start the questioning) and cross examination (defendants' attorney starts the questioning). I know what my goals are for each witness, but I need to turn complicated issues into simple questions and answers. This is an art form. The jurors only see the final "painting" but the amount of thinking, re-thinking and more re-thinking that goes into creating the piece of art known as testimony is very extensive. I always need to keep in mind that the jurors come from all walks of life so the testimony I elicit must be clear, concise and easily understandable to everyone regardless of educational level, work experience or exposure to different fields.

I also need to present the judge at the beginning of the case with my proposal for the legal instructions she/he should read to the jury at the end of evidence. These are very precise legal principles and often times the exact language used by the judge can seriously influence jurors when they hear which laws apply to the facts as they find them. Not every judge is familiar with every law, rule or regulation that applies to each case. It is the duty of the trial attorney to point the judge in the right direction. Often, the opposing lawyers vehemently disagree which direction is the right one.

In addition, I present the judge with my proposed verdict sheet. As the jurors begin their deliberations (when they go back to the jury room to decide your case), they are given a verdict sheet to fill out with answers to specific questions about your case. That sheet is read aloud in open court when deliberations are finished and constitutes the final jury verdict in your case. I make suggestions to the judge how to phrase the questions and instructions that the jurors must follow when filling out the sheet. Jurors are not familiar with verdict sheets since no one uses them in daily living except jurors who are chosen for service (at most, a few times in their lifetimes). It is essential that the sheet is clear, concise and easy to fill out. I have had many an argument with judges and adversaries (defense attorneys) about the composition of these sheets. Even if everything went swimmingly throughout the trial, if the jurors misinterpret the verdict sheet and make inadvertent mistakes in filling it out, your case may be lost forever (It is almost unheard of for courts to overturn jury verdicts when jurors later tell lawyers they misunderstood the verdict sheet and meant to render a different final result).

My final pre-trial to do's are writing up a jury selection introduction and questions as well as an opening statement. I walk into jury selection with the defense attorneys into a room of 20-35 strangers who were summoned to come down to serve jury duty in the county in which they reside. They know nothing about your case and I know nothing about them. My very brief (required by court rules) introduction and questioning of them must be targeted, focused and designed to elicit responses that allow me to decide if they will be good jurors for your case (more about this phase later). A lot of thought goes into my preparation for jury selection. The actual selection process taps into my experience and instincts about people in general. It is pure art, not science.

Finally, I need to have my opening statement written and rehearsed (no good lawyer wings it without practicing an opening out loud). I search my mind for a theme. I make sure the opening statement is concise, cogent, simple, informative and engaging. I need to set the tone for the rest of the trial without making promises about testimony that I can't keep. Trials are filled with surprises such as better than expected witnesses, worse than expected witnesses, surefire good evidence that the judge doesn't let into evidence, legal rulings that make no sense to me but are the final word of the judge and arguments by adversaries that may seem contorted to me but sometimes capture the imagination of jurors. Due to the above potential surprises, I can only promise testimony and evidence in an opening that are 100% certain will come before the jury. My credibility is at stake if I make promises in the opening and don't deliver by the end of the testimony. The opening needs to be measured but persuasive. It may sound easy, but after 37 years of giving openings I know it is a very complicated and difficult task to hit just the right note before the jury for your unique case.

To get back to the boxing analogy, all of the above preparation is 90% of the trial effort. The actual main event in my ring, the courtroom, is all the crowd (jury) sees, but never has a case or boxing match been won solely during the fight (trial). The innumerable hours of unseen and unheard preparation are the secret weapons behind every courtroom and boxing ring victory. Take that to the bank.

The Trial

The vast majority of civil cases (non-criminal cases such as personal injury/medical malpractice, contract disputes, business disputes, etc.) do not go to verdict or even jury selection. There are so many unique things about your case that it is impossible to predict if your personal injury/medical malpractice case will settle before trial, settle at trial or go to verdict. The experienced trial lawyer knows to prepare every case as if it is going to verdict and every hour I spend in pre-trial preparation will pay off in either a fair settlement or a trial I can be proud of when all is said and done. **Hint - if your case does go to trial make sure that your lawyer is a trial lawyer in more than name only. A very small percentage of lawyers actually have extensive experience trying cases. Not only do I try cases for my own clients, but other firms who do not concentrate in trial work hire me on a case-by-case basis to try cases for their clients. Trying a case is all-consuming, incredibly intense and never predictable. It is not an arena for amateurs.**

So, I show up at court and the judge finally says, "go out and pick". That means it is actually, finally, really time to begin jury selection. Well, almost. Sometimes when I report to the jury clerk there are rooms and jurors available. Other times I wait hours or even days for available jurors. I am very used to waiting, rushing, then waiting again as it is the norm in the court system in New York. Patience is another skill that trial lawyers need to have at all times.

Jury Selection

The lawyers, without their clients, go into a room (rarely in a courtroom and rarely with a judge present in the New York state court system) to give a very brief speech on what they intend to prove and their legal positions. Then they question the potential jurors one by one. Each lawyer gets a certain number of challenges (the opportunity to remove a potential juror without giving any reason) while other jurors may be stricken from the panel for a variety of legal reasons.

Some lawyers consider this part of the process tedious and pro forma (like a standard formula). **I consider jury selection to be the most important part of the trial.** I can have the greatest witnesses. I can have the greatest evidence. I can make brilliant arguments in my opening statement and summation. If I have biased people on the jury who are not open, fair, just, focused and willing to judge the case only on the evidence in the courtroom, everything else is useless. Who hears and decides your case is everything at trial.

If you have jurors that hate lawsuits, hate lawyers and hate

> I consider jury selection to be the most important part of the trial.

people in your position (e.g. a bicyclist or taxi driver), the most masterfully presented trial will probably never be enough to overcome their prejudices. I do everything within my power under the rules to find a jury that will give my client's case a fair shake. With a limited number of challenges (times that I can dismiss jurors) it is not always possible to pick a fair jury panel. This becomes more difficult in certain counties where a higher percentage of jurors come in with biases, prejudices and pre-conceived notions about the case they may sit on. As you may recall from earlier, jury selection is art not science. I rely on my experience in many, many jury selections and my ability to size up the fairness of people in a very short time span. Not every judgment made by trial lawyers in jury selection turns out to be right, but every selection must be made based on my instinct and the limited information I can collect by questioning, conversing with and observing the potential jurors in the room. It's like speed dating with legal consequences.

From Opening Statement to Verdict

I could write a whole book about the trial itself (maybe I will if you like this book) since a trial is part informational, part entertainment (I need to keep jurors interested), part inspirational, part intellectual and part emotional (jurors who bond with witnesses, lawyers and the subject matter are much more likely to give your position the benefit of the doubt).

Briefly, once a jury is selected and sworn, the judge, jury, lawyers and parties (usually only the plaintiff to begin the trial) convene in a courtroom. The judge gives his/her opening instructions about the process to the jury. These are quite general instructions to orient the jurors to the procedures that will govern the trial.

The opening statements by the lawyers are then made to the jurors. I go first on behalf of the plaintiff followed by the defense attorneys. As I discussed earlier, this is my first opportunity to speak to the jurors beyond the very short discussions we have during jury selection. I have a chance to give the jurors a road map, present an outline of the expected evidence and let the jurors know why your case is strong and why your arguments should prevail. The opening statement styles of the lawyers are as different as the people presenting them. These openings are very important since it is the first time the jury is oriented toward your version of the case in detail.

The trial continues with the plaintiff's lawyer's presentation of witnesses, documents and other evidence first. The defense lawyers get to cross examine each of my witnesses to try to shake her/his testimony.

After the plaintiff rests (tells the judge there are no more witnesses or evidence on behalf of the plaintiff), the defense lawyers present the defendants' case at which time

I get to do cross-examination of witnesses. Due to scheduling conflicts, a judge may allow a plaintiff or defendant to call a witness out of order, i.e., during the presentation of the opposing lawyer's case.

During testimony, you will hear objections by the lawyers to certain questions, rulings by judges ("overruled" means answer the question, "sustained" means don't answer the question) and admonishments by court reporters (everything is recorded by a court reporter just like on TV) to witnesses to "speak up, please".

When all of the evidence is in, the lawyers make closing arguments (summations). The defendant goes first, and the plaintiff gets the final word in state court in New York. This is every lawyer's final opportunity to speak to the jury, to review the evidence with the jury and to persuade the jury for the final time. I spend many hours before summation reviewing the evidence, reviewing the testimony and reviewing my opening statement to craft just the right kind of summation. It must be cogent and logical. It must be comprehensive without being too long to absorb. It must reach the jurors on both the intellectual and the emotional level. Jurors are not robots, they are human. I don't ask for their sympathy since that is not a permissible element of damages. I do ask for their openness. I do ask for their fairness. I do ask for them to do justice which is a human task not a mechanical formula.

At the end of summation, the judge gives the jurors legal instructions and sends them to their deliberation room with a verdict sheet to fill out with questions about negligence and amounts of money damages. The jurors can take minutes (usually a bad sign for a plaintiff), hours or even multiple days. No one can predict how long a jury will be out or what verdict they will render.

After the jurors finish deliberations and fill out the verdict sheet they are ushered back into the courtroom by the court officer to read the verdict out loud (done by the jury foreperson after the questions are read out loud by the court clerk). We all take deep breaths when they come back because their body language, facial expressions and total time deliberating cannot be read as predictors of their verdict. **Show me a lawyer who tells you they can predict jury verdicts and I'll show you a lawyer who has never tried a case.** The verdict is announced, the judge dismisses the jury and on occasion the jurors talk to the lawyers inside or outside the courthouse about their verdict and deliberations.

Sometimes the lawyers make motions to the judge to set aside the verdict. Judges usually reserve those decisions for a later time and a possible future hearing. When you are on the losing side of the verdict it is rare to get the judge to throw out the verdict.

One side rejoices. One side just keeps shaking its head. The opposing lawyers shake hands. Justice is not always done in everyone's view but the opportunity at justice is given to both sides. If you win as a plaintiff, you love the system, you love your lawyer, you love the jury. If you lose, not so much.

The reality is that jurors are human beings and all of the frailties of humans are on display with the jury. I believe they always do their best to do the right thing. Sometimes they do and sometimes they don't. It depends on which side of the verdict you sit. The risk of every jury trial is the same. Someone wins. Someone loses. No one knows the winner before it is announced. It is very much like a boxing match decided by the judges on points as opposed to a knockout. We can disagree with the boxing judges for eternity, but their decision stands. Sometimes, that deciding factor is just plain good luck. A former NFL great, linebacker Jack Youngblood, is often credited with one of my favorite sayings, "Good luck is a residue of preparation"

There are two exceptions to this being the end of the case. One is the rare instance when the judge throws out the verdict on legal grounds (She/he also has the opportunity to take issues away from the jury at the end of the plaintiff's and defendants' presentation of evidence but that is also rare). The other possibility is if an appeal is taken by the losing side. No one should count on getting a reversal of the verdict or a new trial on appeal since the vast majority of cases are affirmed (the result is kept in place), so the odds on appeal are stacked against the party who loses at trial. Also, there must be defined legal issues that support an appeal. Simply disagreeing with the jury's factual findings is not a basis for appeal. Generally, legal rulings by the trial judge are the usual bases for an appeal.

I have written many briefs and argued many appeals over the years. Appellate courts are not there to substitute their factual opinions for the opinions of the jury. Jurors' verdicts are given great latitude and deference since they are the ultimate finders of fact, not the judge. The appellate courts are most interested in determining if a trial was conducted fairly and in conformity with settled legal principles. Issues of credibility, conflicting versions of an accident and evaluation of pain and suffering are in the unique province of the jury to decide with rare exceptions (If the money verdict is excessively high in the court's view, New York appellate judges are not reluctant to reduce verdicts. The converse, increasing money damages, is not the norm at all.)

If my descriptions of trial preparation and trial presentation sounded exhaustive, it is actually the opposite. My description doesn't begin to tell a trial lawyer's life of waking up in the middle of many nights to write down a new thought or theory. It doesn't do justice to the physical rigors of preparing with a boxer's intensity day after day, month after month until you figuratively walk from the dressing room, through the tunnel and into the ring with the spotlight on you at every moment. A boxer, even an all-time champion, has those butterflies right before getting in the ring before the first punch is thrown and so does the trial lawyer (even after 37 years in the court-room ring) before the opening statement. There is never certainty in the ring no matter how prepared or skilled the boxer has been in the past. In boxing, a lucky punch, a cut over the eye, a poor referee, a questionable judge or a pulled muscle in the third round can change everything in an instant. At a trial, a witness can implode, a doctor can get mixed up on cross-examination, a judge can make strange and harmful rulings, surefire favorable evidence can get excluded by the judge or a jury can just plain not like a party or believe a witness that sounded so credible to me. The trial lawyer, like the boxer, has to be ready for surprise after surprise because things change on a dime at a trial. Expect the unexpected. Plan A never happens so plans B, C, D, E and F better be in your repertoire as a trial lawyer. Thinking on your feet is every good trial lawyer's indispensable skill. It is your credo because rarely do things go as expected. **In the brilliant words of Mike Tyson** (I met him on a line in federal court once and he was a perfect gentlemen and quite engaging), **"Everyone has a plan until they get punched in the mouth"**. No truer words apply to boxing matches and trials.

That sums up the basic stages of a personal injury/medical malpractice trial from my point of view. Next, I need to tell you about your role in the case. It's your case so you better understand what your lawyer expects from you. Leave the legal work to your lawyer. Take care of your own work because only you can do that part. Let's go.

three
The Client's Role in a Lawsuit - **You**

Your role in a personal injury/medical malpractice lawsuit can be summed in 3 strict rules I lay down for every client in preparation for her/his examination before trial testimony and trial testimony:

RULE NO. 1 - TELL THE TRUTH
RULE NO. 2 - TELL THE TRUTH
RULE NO. 3 - TELL THE TRUTH

If you follow those 3 rules at every stage of the lawsuit you have done your job flawlessly.

We live during times when lies, misrepresentations and falsehoods are shrugged off by over 40% of the voting public. That's a disgrace but a theme for another book (I think I'm up to 2 more manuscripts now). Honesty is not just a defining value in living one's life with integrity, but it is the sacred foundation of a fair and just legal system. You will affirm or swear to tell the truth at your examination before trial and, if your case goes to trial, on the witness stand in a courtroom. Your word is gold (or certainly should be) in your everyday interactions with family, friends, business colleagues, acquaintances and strangers. It becomes more precious than gold when you enter the legal system. It becomes a legal obligation and dishonesty under oath in a lawsuit could lead to criminal charges of perjury. Is that scary enough for you to understand that the truth is your only choice at every stage of your lawsuit?

Many people get their legal knowledge from TV shows, movies and books. Some think that they need to say certain things to "help" their cases. **TOTALLY WRONG AND LIKELY ILLEGAL.** Never embellish your injuries, never misrepresent what happened to cause the accident, never shade the truth about your physical limitations in activities or the workplace as the result of the accident. I will put up with a lot of unfortunate things that clients inadvertently do or say during their lawsuits (mixing up address locations, forgetting relevant details, missing scheduled appointments with me or doctors, etc.). **I WILL NEVER PUT UP WITH CLIENTS THAT DO NOT TELL THE TRUTH. PERIOD. STOP.**

You need to tell me (or my investigator if you meet with him first) the whole truth in response to questions about the happening of the accident and your injuries. Not partial truths. Not what you think I want to hear. Just the truth—plain and simple.

My job is to present the truth in the best light possible to insurance companies, defense lawyers, mediators, judges and juries. Despite what you might see in the movies or on TV (not good sources generally), part of my job is never to perpetuate that which is false. Never ask me to do that if you want me as your lawyer. Never hold out on me when I ask you questions. Never let me find out from insurance companies and defense attorneys that you weren't straight with me and have it come as a complete surprise to me that the insurance company has the documented goods on you.

We are living **in an age of unprecedented technological advances.** We are also living in an age, unfortunately, where privacy is threatened in every sector of our lives. All of this means that **virtually everything you do and say relating to your accident is verifiable.** If you deny you had prior accidents with similar injuries, the insurance company is going to do a databank search (There is a national insurance claim databank subscribed to by all insurance companies.) that will find a record of that prior accident, prior similar injury and prior lawsuit.

If you think you can fool the system by claiming you are not working or not

> Never embellish your injuries, never misrepresent what happened to cause the accident, never shade the truth about your physical limitations.

65

engaging in physical activities that you did before the accident, think again. Video surveillance was an expensive proposition when I started practicing law in the early 1980's. Now, it is easy, cheap and part of every insurance investigator's checklist. Always assume you are under video surveillance during your lawsuit. It is legal. It is common. It is just what insurance companies do in any fairly substantial case. Surveillance should not be a problem if you tell your lawyer the truth and testify truthfully during your case. If you're really not working, no one can tape you working. If you're really not playing basketball or jogging, no one can tape you doing that. If you're really not dancing at clubs, no one can tape you dancing.

You know what else insurance companies use to catch you in lies? Your own social media. When you post on Instagram or Facebook photos of you water skiing in Hawaii, you better have testified that you took a vacation to Hawaii and were able to participate in water skiing. If your Instagram shows you in the New York City Marathon, you better not have testified you use a cane at all times. None of this matters if you tell the truth. All of this matters if you lie and it will destroy your case if you are not telling the truth.

STAY OFF OF SOCIAL MEDIA COMPLETELY AFTER YOUR ACCIDENT. You may just be making innocent comments about your accident or injuries that can be misconstrued by defense attorneys and juries. You may be posting what you consider harmless photos of you standing next to friends at a beach volleyball game as a spectator, but the defense may use them to insinuate that you were engaging in beach volleyball as a player. The courts are getting more and more open to the required turnover of your social media postings to the defense. Just stay off social media during your lawsuit, but never delete any posts you made after the accident. That could be considered a fraudulent act even if done innocently, so just don't do it.

DID I ALREADY SAY NEVER EMBELLISH ANYTHING IN A LAWSUIT? It cannot be said to clients enough times. If I accepted your case it means that based on what you told me I believe we have a reasonable chance of establishing liability (fault) on the defendant and I think your injuries are substantial enough to merit my time, money and effort on your behalf. Since I charge a contingency fee, if you lose, I lose. No win, no legal fee. It is my pleasure to represent you as long as you have told me the truth.

The worst thing you can do as a client is to exaggerate the impact of a crash, exaggerate the depth of a sidewalk defect or exaggerate the pain and disabilities caused by your injuries. Let me persuade insurance adjusters, defense attorney and jurors about the merits of your case. You just tell the truth and I'll present the truth in the best light possible to try to maximize your recovery. **The moment you embellish or exaggerate is the moment your case starts to sink. Don't think it. Don't say it. Don't do it.**

Your participation in the lawsuit will be needed relatively few times over the course of the lawsuit. After our initial meeting (Hopefully, you reported the incident to the police, and you have the police report with you when you retain a lawyer) you need to keep my office current on any medical updates or new medical providers. You need to keep my office current of any changes in missed work time and lost wages.

Other than those obligations, you will be notified by my office when we need you to do certain things. You will be notified of a prep time with me before examinations before trial (always subject to change due to last minute postponements of examinations before trial for innumerable reasons). You will be notified about the time and place to meet me to give your testimony at the examination before trial.

You will be contacted by my office about scheduled appointments with doctors designated by defendants and doctors retained by us (if your treating doctor is not doing a narrative report and testifying at trial). You will be contacted by us if we need you to be present during an engineering/safety expert's examination of a location or defect.

If the case goes to a mediation (a settlement conference at a private mediation company), we will contact you about the schedule and require you to be present.

Finally, if the case goes to trial, we will tell you when to come in for the trial prep. At the trial itself you are expected to be there daily for the entire trial which can last days or weeks depending on so many factors that are out of my control.

If the case settles, you are expected to come to my office to sign the appropriate documents to settle your case. You will have the choice of having your share of the settlement monies mailed to you or coming into my office to pick up the check.

You are always welcome to call me or schedule an appointment at any stage of your case. I am happy to provide answers to your questions as the case proceeds.

As you can see, the chapter about your duties is much shorter than the chapter about my duties. That page difference accurately reflects the time and effort each of us has to put into your lawsuit.

If you are my client, then your life has been disrupted by a terrible accident or medical malpractice. Your work life or family life have been upended. Your physical state has been seriously compromised by the injuries you incurred. You have lots on your mind due to this unfortunate upheaval thrust upon you through no fault of your own.

You hired me to carry the burden of fighting for your rights. You hired me to spar with insurance adjusters, defense attorneys and judges. You hired me to persuade jurors if we go to trial. You hired me to convey the message to all of the above that you were hurt due to the negligence of others. You were hurt so seriously that your pain and suffering is permanent. You were badly hurt, and your life was shattered in ways big and small. You hired me to be your voice, to argue your case and to stand up for your rights. You hired me to fight for you, counsel you and advise you. You hired me to do all the necessary and detailed legal work to put your case in the best position possible to maximize your recovery by way of settlement or verdict.

That is why the workload, the time and the effort put into your case falls almost entirely on me once you retain me as your lawyer. Your job is to restore your health and life to the best it can be under the awful circumstances of being a victim of a serious accident or medical malpractice. I'll call you when I need you, but you hired me to lift the burden of waging the battle to get you justice for what happened to you. Let me carry that burden while you rebuild your life.

When critical times arise in your case (examination before trial testimony, settlement offers, mediation, trial testimony preparation or the trial itself), you don't have to worry about hearing from me. You and I will have the discussions and meetings we need to have. Ask your questions, clarify my answers, get all the information you want from me. The vast majority of your time as the case progresses will be spent waiting for the case to inch toward its conclusion. Any lawyer who tells you that the system is quick and the results come fast is being a salesperson, not a lawyer. The courts in New York are constantly backlogged. Court conferences, examinations before trial, motions (applications to the court for various legal relief) and trial dates get adjourned regularly for months at a time as a matter of course. I cannot promise you that the justice system is quick. It is quite slow. Go about your life and be patient about your lawsuit. Given the choice, you really do want an opportunity at the justice system getting it right rather than getting it over with quickly. As hard as it will seem, **BE PATIENT.**

Any lawyer who tells you that the system is quick, and the results come fast is being a salesperson, not a lawyer.

four
My Pledge

Rest assured that I will give your case the utmost care, attention and effort it deserves. You are my client. I take our relationship very seriously. I have an ethical duty to zealously represent you at every phase of the case. I will uphold my duty. It is an honor to represent my clients. I never forget that. Not for a single minute. Not once since 1982 have I not put every ounce of my energy into a client's case. You, the victim of someone else's negligence, are why I do what I do. I love what I do. I believe in what I do. I value my reputation, my honesty, my integrity, my dedication and my compassion for those who have taken hard knocks in life. I take great pride in fighting for regular people against large corporations, giant hospitals, bad landlords, large New York City agencies and insurance company behemoths.

No lawyer can guarantee results. That wouldn't be honest. I can, however, pledge that I will do everything in my power to put your case in the best position possible to be successful.

To finish with another boxing analogy (I do love boxing), when the fight is over, I leave every last ounce of sweat in the ring. That I can assure you.

I take great pride in fighting for regular people against large corporations, giant hospitals, bad landlords, large New York City agencies and insurance company behemoths.

five
About the Author

Richard C. Bell has been practicing law in New York City since 1982. In 1986, he opened his own practice focused on personal injury and medical malpractice and he has maintained that practice based in Manhattan since that time. He represents clients in cases resulting from negligence, including auto accidents, construction accidents, medical malpractice, police brutality, nursing home negligence, falldowns, product liability and more. Mr. Bell handles all aspects of his cases, from the initial investigation through settlement, trial verdict and appeal. He is motivated by a true sense of concern for his clients and a desire to get them the compensation they deserve by fighting to make sure those responsible are brought to justice. Though he is a tough trial attorney, he treats his clients with respect and compassion because he understands the personal tumult they are experiencing.

Mr. Bell graduated Magna Cum Laude from Duke University. He then received his Juris Doctor from Rutgers University School of Law. While at Rutgers, he served as the Features Editor for the Rutgers Journal of Computers, Technology, and the Law and was a member of the Rutgers Moot Court Board. Upon graduation, he was admitted to the New York Bar as well as the New Jersey Bar. After working for numerous law firms, in 1986 he opened his own practice focusing on plaintiffs' personal injury and medical malpractice law. He has also been admitted to the U.S. District Court – Southern District of New York, Eastern District of New York, Northern District of New York and District of New Jersey. He is a member of the New York State Trial Lawyers Association and the New York State Bar Association.

Mr. Bell has also participated in speaking engagements about personal injury law at a number of prestigious conferences in Barcelona, Cancun, San Francisco and Washington, D.C. He has also been honored by Super Lawyers, The Million Dollar Advocates Forum, National Academy of Personal Injury Attorneys and Top Attorneys of North America.

Significant Cases

Mr. Bell has a history of success at trial and in settlement negotiations.[*] Some of his significant cases include:

- A $8 million verdict in an automobile/truck accident case
- A $6.5 million verdict in a urological medical malpractice case
- A $3.6 million settlement in an auto accident and road maintenance case after five weeks of trial

---

[*]   Prior results cannot and do not guarantee a similar outcome.

- A $2.9 million settlement against 12 defendants in a medical malpractice and wrongful death suit
- A $2.7 million verdict in a case concerning a woodworking machine in a prison
- A $2.5 million settlement at jury selection in a premises liability case
- A $2.325 million settlement in a construction worker accident
- A $1.3 million settlement for trip and fall by a truck driver on a loading dock

He has handled a number of high profile cases that were featured on The Donahue Show, WINS Radio, WMCA Radio and appeared in the *New York Times, Daily News, New York Post, The Staten Island Advance, Jet Magazine, The New York Law Journal, The New York Jury Verdict Reporter* and *The Atla Law Reporter.*

Community involvement

Mr. Bell is not only dedicated to the good of his clients, he is also committed to serving the community as a whole. To this end, he has done extensive pro bono work (free legal work in the public interest), including representing the estate of a 9/11 victim before the Federal September 11th Victim Compensation Fund through the Trial Lawyers Care organization. He has also been recognized by the New York Firefighter's Burn Center Foundation for pro bono work. **Mr. Bell is passionate about protecting voting rights.** He has served as a pro bono attorney for a number of years representing individual voters on Election Day in New Jersey applying for court orders to overturn decisions by election poll officials who rescinded their right to vote. He also advised voters at polling places in Cleveland, Ohio, Philadelphia, Pennsylvania and Fort Lauderdale, Florida about their voting rights on Election Day from 2004 to the present. He believes every citizen should be registered to vote, every registered voter should be allowed to vote and every vote should be counted at every polling place in America. An assault on voting rights is an assault on our democracy. It is an assault on our freedom. **As Dr. Martin Luther King once said, "Voting is the foundation stone for political action". His fellow civil rights and voting rights crusader, Fannie Lou Hamer, reminded us, "Nobody is free until everybody is free".**

In his personal injury/medical malpractice law practice, his professional goal is to provide tenacious representation for his clients to get them the financial compensation they deserve and to help them bring closure to a traumatic time in their lives. To learn more about Mr. Bell and how he may be able to help you, call him toll free at (877) CALL-LAW (225-5529) or call 212.714.0988. Check out his website at www.877calllaw.com. He offers a free initial consultation and once he has determined that you have a viable personal injury or medical malpractice case and you enter into a written retainer agreement with him, he can begin a detailed investigation and prepare to effectively pursue your case.*

---

*   Prior results cannot and do not guarantee a similar outcome.

THE LAW OFFICES OF

RICHARD C. BELL

545 8th Avenue, 8th Floor
New York, NY 10018

(877) CALL-LAW
www.877calllaw.com

WA

www.ingramcontent.com/pod-product-compliance
Lightning Source LLC
Chambersburg PA
CBHW071113210326
41519CB00020B/6284